STEPHANIE DINKINS

ON LOVE & DATA

Edited by Srimoyee Mitra
Stamps Gallery,
Penny W. Stamps School of Art & Design,
University of Michigan Press • Ann Arbor

Published in the United States of America
by the University of Michigan Press
Manufactured in Canada
Printed on acid-free paper

First published February 2024

A CIP catalog record for this book is available
from the British Library.

Library of Congress Cataloging-in-Publication
data has been applied for.

ISBN 978-0-472-03959-3 (paper : alk. paper)
ISBN 978-0-472-90399-3 (open access ebook)
DOI: https://doi.org/10.3998/mpub.12742314

The publisher gratefully acknowledges the support
of Andy Warhol Foundation for the Visual
Arts and the Penny W. Stamps School of Art
& Design for making this book possible.

The University of Michigan Press's open access
publishing program is made possible thanks
to additional funding from the University of Michigan
Office of the Provost and the generous support
of contributing libraries.

Srimoyee Mitra
Editor

Nancy Niles
Copy Editor

Jennifer Junkermeier-Khan
Project Assistant

Kikko Paradela and Emily Anderson
Design

Cover Images
Stephanie Dinkins
Secret Garden, 2021
Screen grab from Secret Garden
WebXR online
© Stephanie Dinkins

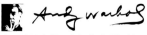

Foreword

Framework

Essays

Table of Contents

On Love & Data:
A Foreword

Salome Asega

3   Sarah Elizabeth Lewis, "The Racial Bias Built into Photography," *New York Times*, April 25, 2019, https://www.nytimes.com/2019/04/25/lens/sarah-lewis-racial-bias-photography.html.

4   "The Black Reconstruction Collective on the Architecture of Equity," *Deem Journal*, https://www.deemjournal.com/stories/brc.

1   Toni Morrison, *The Bluest Eye* (New York: Holt, Rinehart and Winston, 1970).

2   Imamu Amiri Baraka, "The Book of Life," in *Raise, Race, Rays, Raze: Essays since 1965* (New York: Random House, 1971), http://www.soulsista.com/titanic/baraka.html.

Stephanie Dinkins
Not the Only One Avatar: Becoming, 2020
Digital image
© Stephanie Dinkins

Our maker-sister Stephanie Dinkins presents to us a stunning collection of works delicately bound by this title *On Love & Data*—a bold interpolation of feeling and measurement. I think at once of Toni Morrison writing, "Love is never any better than the lover"[1] and also Amira Baraka writing, "Machines are an extension of their inventor-creators."[2] Both love and data radiate from points, from People, and for as long as I can remember, Stephanie Dinkins has been reminding us that we, the People, are wrapped up in the making and reading of artificial intelligence systems.

An artist, a creative technologist, an educator, a researcher, a spacemaker, a mentor, a collaborator, a time traveler. Stephanie wears all the hats. I first learned of her work in 2012 while doing research for an exhibition exploring the private language embodied in cultural time. Even then, Stephanie had a sharp proclamation on time and had a rigorous sculpture and video practice exploring how history could help shape shared definitions for future generations, a theme I see continued in her Afro-now-ism concept. The stories we pass down about each other become their own kind of code or algorithm, and it is Stephanie's urge for us to take risks, to imagine and define ourselves, and to write our own algorithms. You see her pursuit in time, story algorithms, and self-definition run through many of Stephanie's works. *Secret Garden*, *Not the Only One V1 Beta 2*, and *Say It Aloud* each invite the viewers to become participants and encourage viewers to reclaim their individual power and agency to name, determine, and anticipate on their own terms.

And while much of Stephanie's work has a playful invitation to participate, there is also a seriousness that posits, "Can you afford not to engage?" Isn't it urgent, reader, that we craft the technology into tools for support and care? As Stephanie has a background in photo-based practices, I point to photography as an example of another form that floated between science and art. Early critics thought photography was a means for painters to document landscapes and people that they could later artfully reinterpret with paintbrush. The camera was seen as objective and neutral, but we've obviously come to understand it so differently now. Professor and writer Sarah Elizabeth Lewis writes it so simply, "Photography is not just a system of calibrating light, but a technology of subjective decisions."[3] Stephanie's work is about highlighting the subjectivity and reconstructing AI architecture as much as it is about reclamation of our own data in these systems. Artist V. Mitch Mcewen, a member of the Black Reconstructions Collective, a group of Black architects, describes reconstructing as implying deconstructing, rethinking, and determining who is responsible for imagining the future.[4] As you move through the texts, consider what ideological and institutional shifts are needed to produce a more just architecture that is mindful of race, gender, aging, and our future histories.

It is my sincere hope that this book will provide the reader with a deeper understanding and appreciation for Stephanie's multipronged practice and the impact it has made across disciplines. Each highlighted artwork is a testament to her commitment to exploring new themes and techniques, and her unwavering dedication to community-centered storytelling. This book is a celebration of their achievements and a glimpse into their process. As you move through the texts and images in this book, I hope you acutely consider Stephanie's question, "What does AI need from you?"

Foreword

Stephanie Dinkins
Afro-now-ism, 2021
Installation view, Stamps Gallery, 2021
Neon light
Photo by Eric Bronson, U-M Photography

Afro-now-ism

Stephanie Dinkins

Our systems, institutions, leaders, and narratives about who and what we are—our lack of compassion and limited definitions of what a valued member of society is—are failing us. They have been failing us for quite some time. Both COVID-19 and the uprising against systemic racism based on greed, fear, and territorialism are symptoms making visible the inequities that continually seethe just beneath the surface of "civil society."

At this moment, we are unequivocally confronted with the need to reimagine our humanity and what it means to be living organisms sharing the planet with many other organisms, some living, some not. This is nothing new.

However, at this moment, we can plainly see how black, brown, queer, and disabled bodies are devalued; how people who threaten the comfort of those benefiting from institutional power are expendable. Humans have the responsibility to reconceive the systems that threaten communities rendered simultaneously hyper visible and invisible by their perceived difference.

It is now time to reconstruct the idea of the human. What to include within the concept? What is truly valued? Here I am not referring to what is valuable to you, but valued period.

At stake are dignity, equal rights, and the equitable distribution of resources, as well as the survival of the planet. If this moment of twin pandemics has taught us anything, it's that denying these determinants will negatively impact all but the wealthiest among us sooner than we think.

As artificially intelligent ecosystems based on opaque algorithms and biased data proliferate and biological design gains momentum, we are confronted with the need to reimagine human supremacy. Advances in our understanding of machine learning and our single-celled bacterial cousins portend opportunities to create broad definitions of society based on mutuality and lateral coexistence among species and computational machines.

Before we can truly take advantage of these advances, humans must confront a litany of violences we have enacted upon each other. These include institutional and social constructions of race, caste, class, and gender that build and maintain current systems of power. We must also renegotiate our relationship to the spectrum of living beings deemed beneath human and the machines inching ever closer to autonomy. To (re)imagine and optimize the expectations, values, treaties, and global competitions for the near future, we must recognize, especially in the American context, that our ideals—all men are created equal, for example—are often in direct opposition to our legislated power relations.

It is helpful to imagine these roadblocks as questions: How do we rediscover ourselves anew? How do we right our collective rememory?[1] Think of rememory as an undoing, unraveling, and rewriting of corporeal constitutive elements. In the changingness of rememory, could we find transcendence? Or perhaps a trace of a former history that gives us the opportunity to draft something entirely new?

Most words we have available to think about ourselves as human construct worlds that silently imply a false dichotomy between humans on the one hand and nature and machines on the other. Escaping the recursive futures on the horizon requires understanding ourselves as participants in an expanding continuum of

1 Toni Morrison, "'I Wanted to Carve Out a World Both Culture-Specific and Race-Free': An Essay by Toni Morrison," The Guardian, August 8, 2019.

Framework

intelligences sandwiched between technology (AI, biotech, gene editing, etc.) and a greater understanding of the ancient bacterial systems from which we emanate. Moving toward more expansive and equitable visions of what is and can be demands close examination and reconciliation of our perceived human differences.

Is what we're seeking alternative modalities or protocols for beings and non beings? Preoccupied with the then and later, we find ourselves in the now. "Afro-now-ism" is the spectacular technology of the unencumbered black mind in action. It is a willful practice that imagines the world as one needs it to be to support successful engagement—in the here and now.

Instead of waiting to reach the proverbial promised land, also known as a time in the future that may or may not manifest in your lifetime, Afro-now-ism is taking the leap and the risks to imagine and define oneself beyond systemic oppression. It is active resistance away from cynicism, disaffection, and indifference toward constructively channeling energy today. For black people in particular, it means conceiving yourself in the space of free and expansive thought and acting from a critically integrated space, allowing for more community-sustaining work.

Afro-now-ism also demands that we recognize which ideas are so deeply internalized that we no longer understand them as external. In our recognition and enactment of the future dismantlement of systemic barriers in the present moment, we challenge internalized ideas, which often stop us from acting or doing our best.

It is true these oppressive factors do not disappear from our material reality. But for a time,

the mind can, in the name of self and community care, be less discouraged by outside forces to work toward that which sustains more holistically. Systemic barriers will rear their heads again and again. But the Afro-now-ist is stronger and more immediately generative for having done the work, acted on their deepest hopes and desires without inhibition—today. Exploring where impediments are hard, where they are soft, and when they can be ignored is powerful. Technological enhancements and self-care techniques from the past, present, and future can and should be used to supersede distractions from claiming our sovereignty, wholeness, and propriety.

Afro-now-ism asks how we liberate our minds from the infinite loop of repression and oppositional thinking America imposes upon those of us forcibly enjoined to this nation. What incremental changes do we make to our internal algorithms to lurch our way to ever-more-confident means of thriving in this world? The question is not only what injustices are you fighting against, but what do you in your heart of hearts want to create?

This is a pointed question for black folks but includes the rest of society as well. Our fates, whether we like it or not, acknowledge it or not, are intermingled. Though it is not immediately legible, we sink or swim together. Still, at times, communities need space and time to build, grow, and fortify apart from the whole. That's OK as long as communities find paths to understanding in a kind of complex Venn diagram of trust from which to negotiate our shared futures.

The rapid proliferation of AI into social, political, and cultural contexts provides opportunities to change the way we define and administer crucial social relations and manage resources. Self-organization and complexity hold important cues to how AI can help instantiate equity, cultural richness, and direct governance (or at least broad and direct input into governance). Through AI and the proliferation of smart technologies, everyday people, globally, can help define what the technological future should look like and how it should function, as well as design methods to help achieve our collective goals. Direct input from the public can also help infuse AI ecosystems with nuanced ideas, values, and beliefs toward the equitable distribution of resources and mutually beneficial systems of governance.

Black liberation rests on the construction of a non-oppositional consciousness, unburdened by the need to endlessly challenge the fears, imaginative apprehensions, oppressions, and entanglements of others. The unencumbered, undistracted black mind is a wellspring of possibility. It is a tool and way of being that changes what counts as the black experience in the twenty-first century. This is a struggle over life and death. The boundaries between sovereign consciousness, nature, valued knowledge, biotechnologies, power, and social reality are optical illusions.

The reconstruction of an intersectional black politics requires practices and theory that address the social relations of science and technology, crucially including the systems of myth, power, and time that structure our imaginations. Viewed through blackness, and the lens of the American imaginary, rememory presupposes an excavation of the terrors and joys cultivated in spite of the conditions of a nation built on slavery. We mine, disassemble, reimagine, and call on past, present, and future. We are a protopian collective advancing toward fully empowered communities, personal selves, and others.

These are the selves that the vilified and underutilized must fight for and encode into our inextricably connected future histories. If humans are to make new ways forward in partnership with nature and technology, we must first take a close look at and upend the concepts, histories, institutions, and systems that support the inequitable distribution of resources and power.

Afro-now-ism

Framework

Who are your people?

What do you need to release to move forward?

Radical Love & Data Justice: The Empowering Art of Stephanie Dinkins

Srimoyee Mitra

1   Stephanie Dinkins, #Say It Aloud, 2021.

2   Here I use "poor" to reference Hito Steryl, "In Defense of the Poor Image," e-flux Journal, Issue 10, November 2009, https://www.e-flux.com/journal/10/61362/in-defense-of-the-poor-image/, where she contrasts the poor image, a low-resolution image, imperfect cinema as a defiant image that is more widely distributed, remixed, and interpreted, allowing for contributions from a much larger group of people, in contrast to the "rich" image, which represents corporate power, strict controls, and elitism.

3   Dinkins, #SayItAloud.

4   Dinkins, #SayItAloud.

A dark room. A floating figure in cyberspace. As I walk by, the figure shape-shifts and speaks. She/they ask: "What do you need to release in this world to move forward?"[1]

There is a soundtrack; it is otherworldly, rhythmic, and inviting. I walk deeper into the room, intrigued by the figure, to get a better "view" of the image. The outline of the figure is soft and amorphous, resembling a low-resolution image that one would associate with analog television monitors from back in the day. It is a stark contrast to the crisp and flawless high-definition images I realize I have come to expect. The "poor" image[2] is made up of large, colorful, orb-shaped pixels that are reddish-purple, brown, and silver and in flux, moving and opening up a sense of curiosity—in contrast to the finality of a "rich" image. This is the image of Professor Commander Justice (PCJ), who addresses viewers as they enter the gallery. Her/their gregarious voice and prescient words hold space.

PCJ is the central character in a web extended reality (WebXR) experience and new media installation called #SayItAloud (2021), created by Stephanie Dinkins, whose research and practice weave together art production, exhibition, and workshops with the objective of making artificial intelligence systems more equitable, accessible, and accountable. For her first major survey exhibition, On Love & Data, which was organized by Stamps Gallery at the University of Michigan (2021) and toured to the Queens Museum (2022), Dinkins expanded the solo WebXR experience from the confines of a computer screen to an immersive social experience. It took the form of a two-channel new media installation. When a viewer enters the gallery and exchanges gazes with PCJ on the wall, PCJ begins to interact with them regardless of their cultural, social, or economic background and positionality. PCJ is "eager to spread the word about Afro-now-

ism—a willful practice that imagines the world as one needs it to be to support successful engagement, asserting that the Afro-now-ist is stronger and more immediately generative for having acted on their deepest hopes and desires without inhibition—today."[3] And so, PCJ continues: "The question is not only what injustices you are fighting against, but what do you, in your heart of hearts, want to create in this world."[4] Dinkins's strategy to deny viewers access to a brilliant, high-resolution, "rich" image liberates them from being captivated by it and empowers them to be intentional about their decision and to actively look, listen, and engage with PCJ. Dinkins employs Intel RealSense Technology that enables PCJ to "see" and interact with viewers when they actively engage with her/them. By unlocking new and equitable ways of interacting with the work and with one another in the gallery space, Dinkins fosters a sense of reciprocity between self and other, human and machine, listening and responding.

The viewers' minor gestures and eye movements trigger deeper engagement with PCJ, who will then continue to share her/their ideas about Afro-now-ism and ask each viewer to respond to her/their questions. The projection of the "poor" image continues to shift as teardrop-shaped pods that resemble portals into other worlds—populated with different people speaking, smiling, and looking—float around PCJ's figure. In the center of the room is another space tucked behind velvet curtains—a recording booth where PCJ encourages viewers to contribute their ideas. Each of those video contributions from the public appears in the WebXR environment and adds to an expanding cacophony of voices online and in the public

8 Stephanie Dinkins, "Afro-now-ism: The Unencumbered Black Mind Is a Well-spring of Possibility," NOEMA, June 16, 2020, https://www.noemamag.com/afro-now-ism/.

7 Tommy Martinez, "Towards an Equitable Ecosystem of Artificial Intelligence," broadcast, Pioneer Works, May 15, 2020, https://pioneerworks.org/broadcast/stephanie-dinkins-towards-an-equitable-ecosystem-of-ai.

5 John Byrne, Elinor Morgan, November Paynter, Aida Sanchez de Serdio, Adela Železnik, et al., eds., The Constituent Museum: Constellation of Knowledge, Politics and Mediation (Amsterdam: Valiz, 2018), 11.

6 Byrne et al., The Constituent Museum, 10.

Snapshot of Nana (Bernice Curry) in her garden
From the Dinkins Family photo archive
Reprinted with permission of Stephanie Dinkins

gallery space and proposes new ways in which folks can share space. I was amazed as I watched audience members embrace PCJ's prompts and listen to her words in the space. There was a sense of wonder and community as they watched the contributions of others floating in the teardrop-shaped portals. *Say It Aloud* uses a simple call-and-response pattern as PCJ activates the gallery space and asks every viewer to respond to her/their prompts. These responses are then included in a growing repository of people's ideas advocating and inventing new ways forward. Dinkins makes these responses publicly accessible online and through her installations, cultivating a sense of agency and collectivity among the viewers.

Dinkins's artistic vision resonates with the essential anthology on museum practices, *The Constituent Museum: Constellations of Knowledge, Politics and Mediation: A Generator of Social Change*, where the editors ask: "What would happen if museums put relationships at the center of their operation?"[5] The publication takes the museum visitor as a member of a constituent body whom it facilitates, provokes, and inspires, rather than as a passive receiver of predefined content. By placing the relation to one's constituent at the center of the museum organization, and "by considering a constituent relationship as being one of collaboration and co-production, the relative positions of both the museum and its constituencies begin to shift and change."[6]

Dialogue is a central theme and approach in Dinkins's art practice. Her artworks are platforms for dialogue, where she goes back and forth asking questions based on critical concerns of our time to explore and brainstorm ideas, as solutions to these wicked problems do not yet exist. Through dialogue, Dinkins builds a sustained relationship with the viewer, even if it is temporarily within the gallery space while audiences experience and engage with her work. The call-and-response approach sparks creativity and agency to devise new paths toward outcomes that support and sustain community, starting at home and rippling out nationally and internationally.[7]

During the pandemic, which upended everyday routines and laid bare the deep roots of racial- and gender-based violence against people of color and LGBTQ+ communities, Dinkins published her manifesto and philosophy on the zeitgeist of her art practice, which is included in this volume. The artist explains her inspiration to find solutions to deep-rooted problems that experts all over the world are still grappling with. In the manifesto, she wrote:

> Instead of waiting to reach the proverbial promised land, also known as a time in the future that may or may not manifest in your lifetime, Afro-now-ism is taking the leap and the risks to imagine and define oneself beyond systemic oppression. . . . For black people in particular, it means conceiving yourself in the space of free and expansive thought and acting from a critically integrated space, allowing for more community-sustaining work.[8]

During this time, Dinkins created a series of powerful works such as *Secret Garden* (2021–), an immersive installation and web experience illuminating the power and resilience of Black women that was originally commissioned by New Inc and the Onassis Foundation, debuted at Sundance Film Festival's *New Frontier* in 2022, and was

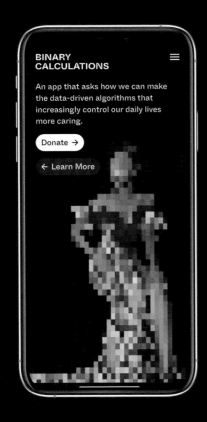

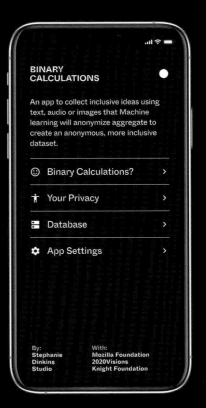

Stephanie Dinkins
*Binary Calculations Are Inadequate
to Assess Us*, 2021
Mobile app, screen grabs, dimensions variable
© Stephanie Dinkins

9   Stephanie Dinkins, interview by Srimoyee
      Mitra, June 20, 2022.

10   Stephanie Dinkins, artist statement, 2020.

restaged for her survey exhibition *On Love & Data* later that year. The viewer is invited to step inside a garden and encounter oral histories of Black women spanning generations. As visitors move about in the installation, they encounter these stories—among them surviving a slave ship, growing up on a Black-owned farm in the 1920s, surviving 9/11, and embodying an avatar powered by African American women. Some of the stories are based on Dinkins's own history. *Secret Garden* reminds viewers that our stories are our algorithms, and that sharing and remembering them are acts of resistance and solidarity. Dinkins credits her grandmother as the inspiration behind this work and for the concept of Afro-now-ism that guides her practice. She states:

I grew up in Tottenville in Staten Island. It is on the southernmost tip of New York and is more like a provincial town than a New York City neighborhood. A small enclave of Black families lived there and, for the most part, they were relegated to a place called "the flats," a small apartment complex on the edge of town. (I learned much later it was one of few places in town that would rent to Black families.) Nana made the best of that situation, turning the large dirt lot on the side of the building into a vibrant garden that she kept meticulously manicured, attracting admirers from around the neighborhood. They would walk by, admire the garden, and eventually talk to her. I now realize the garden was a form of social practice. She enchanted and seduced even her most trenchant white neighbors with the garden's beauty. Her work in that garden—her joy really—helped make Black families living in the area safer and more comfortable. The garden was a space of social practice that built alliances which ultimately granted her solace and entry into the community. That garden was vital to the way I think about working in, and building, community. My projects are most gratifying when they have an underlying use value.[9]

Through her inquiry-based practice exploring emerging technologies, Dinkins recognizes that twenty-first-century society is becoming more and more reliant on AI systems. Yet the algorithms they are built on and the data that inform them are dated and deeply biased. In her artist statement she writes that as society becomes more and more reliant on AI and algorithms, people of color, people with disabilities, LGBTQ+ people, and other marginalized communities must participate in the creation, training, and testing of the algorithmic matrices that currently appraise, assist, and diagnose us, and will do so with ever-increasing consequences in the future."[10] This led Dinkins to develop *Binary Calculations Are Inadequate to Assess Us*, or *BCAI*, an app to examine the exclusionary nature of AI and the algorithms that undergird our technologies, as well as the steps we can take to create more equitable data sets. *BCAI* debuted in Dinkins's survey exhibition and resonates with the abolitionist mission of Data for Black Lives, a movement of activists, organizers, and mathematicians committed to the mission of using data science to create concrete and measurable change in the lives of Black people. While on one hand they agree with data scientists that data have the potential to drive public good and empower communities of color and those who have been systematically marginalized, they caution that missing and misused data can undermine the benefits that data-driven technologies bring to society.[11] Claire Melamed, CEO of the Global Partnership for Sustainable Development Data, suggests that if data are to be part of building a more just world, they must be collected and used freely and independently to tackle the powers that maintain injustice. Likewise, people need to be included in the process of data production, collection, and use—to be counted in the ways that matter most in explaining the unique realities they face.[12]

BCAI is an experiment and exploration of what it takes to build a data set from scratch, rather than relying solely on Big Data that is owned by a handful of multinationals, whose algorithms reinforce inequality and perpetuate injustice. For example, machine-learning systems such as predictive policing, or those that help judges determine the length of jail sentences, or the depth of medical care and so on, are based on historical data that are biased.[13] In contrast, the *BCAI* app asks users to donate images and texts that honor their lives, cultures, and values with details. The user contributions help in building what Dinkins calls a people's data commons that understands and respects diverse, multigenerational communities. The data collected contribute to the *BCAI* app by creating two repositories—one for text and one for images—which were available for people to use as an alternative to existing data sets. At Stamps Gallery, users were invited to participate and test the app, downloaded on iPads placed in voting booths, indicating that ensuring the transparency and governance of AI and machine learning is a shared responsibility between the people, government, and private corporations. In an interview, Dinkins explains:

> Through my artwork I organize workshops. I get people to talk about artificial intelligence (AI) and algorithms: what they are and how they impact our lives. Even those of us who have no ideas, or even an inkling, of what these systems are, can we think about and call out problems we can see in the system? Because if people aren't looking for the follies and calling them out, then they will just get coded deeper and deeper into the system.[14]

Dinkins situates *BCAI* within the social-political (neoliberal) context of our present day by making the app downloadable on Google Play and the Apple Store. Along with the installation, Dinkins runs a workshop to discuss the complex and nuanced decisions and negotiations that must be grappled with in providing data. In this way, Dinkins truly tests out the potential and possibilities that exist within the institutional structures not only of AI and machine learning but also the white cube of a gallery/museum space. The viewer is recast as an active agent of change, a viewer-citizen, who has agency to choose, negotiate, advocate, and refuse to provide their data to *BCAI*, if that is their preference. Dinkins offers viewers a choice, contrary to many Big Data companies that require users to complete tests by providing data in order to access information. In the gallery, *BCAI* drew attention to the fact that galleries and museums are not neutral spaces, and must confront their own histories of white supremacy and exclusion. She reminds the viewer and public audience that they have agency to demand transparency, equity, and inclusion from their cultural institutions.

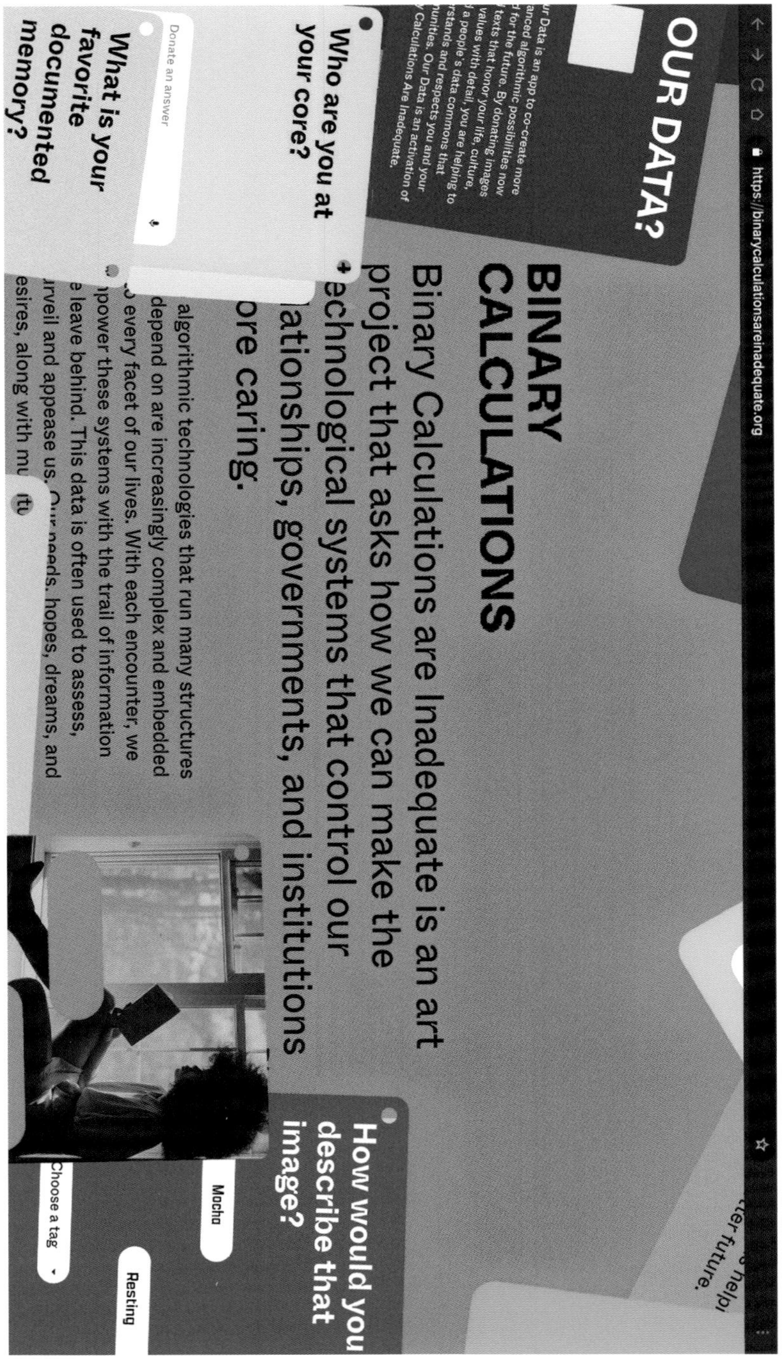

OUR DATA?

ur Data is an app to co-create more
anced algorithmic possibilities now
d for the future. By donating images
 texts that honor your life, culture,
values with detail, you are helping to
d a people's data commons that
rstands and respects you and your
nunities. Our Data is an activation of
y Calculations Are Inadequate.

Who are you at
your core?

Donate an answer

What is your
favorite
documented
memory?

**BINARY
CALCULATIONS**

Binary Calculations are Inadequate is an art
project that asks how we can make the
echnological systems that control our
lationships, governments, and institutions
ore caring.

 algorithmic technologies that run many structures
 depend on are increasingly complex and embedded
o every facet of our lives. With each encounter, we
mpower these systems with the trail of information
e leave behind. This data is often used to assess,
urveil and appease us. Our needs, hopes, dreams, and
esires, along with mu tu

How would you
describe that
image?

Mocha

Resting

Choose a tag

Stephanie Dinkins
*Binary Calculations Are Inadequate
to Assess Us*, 2021
Screen grab
© Stephanie Dinkins
The reading woman image is a photo
by Thought Catalog on Unsplash.
This is a FREE stock image from Unsplash.
See Unsplash License.

11   Data for Black Lives, "About,"
     https://d4bl.org/about.

12   Ada Lovelace Institute, "Black Data Matters:
     How Mission Data Undermines Equitable
     Societies," virtual event, September 9, 2020,
     https://www.adalovelaceinstitute.org/event/
     black-data-matters-how-missing-data-under-
     mines-equitable-societies/.

13   Julia Angwin, Jeff Larson, Surya Mattu, and
     Lauren Kirchner, "Machine Bias," *ProPublica*,
     May 23, 2016, https://www.propublica.
     org/article/machine-bias-risk-assess-
     ments-in-criminal-sentencing.

14   Stephanie Dinkins, interview.

15 Amy Goodman, "Freedom Struggle: Angela Davis on Calls to Defund Police, Racism & Capitalism, and the 2020 Election," *Democracy Now!*, September 7, 2020, https://www.democracynow.org/2020/9/7/freedom_struggle_angela_davis_on_calls.

16 Arundhati Roy, "Arundhati Roy: The Pandemic Is a Portal," *Financial Times*, April 3, 2020, https://www.ft.com/content/10d8f5e8-74eb-11ea-95fe-fcd274e920ca.

17 Srimoyee Mitra, "Curating Catalysts for Social Change," Public 64: *Beyond Settling*.

18 Byrne et al. *The Constituent Museum*, 9, 10.

Stephanie Dinkins #SayItAloud, 2020–21 Interactive WebXR experience (https://sayitaloud.stephaniedinkins.com/) © Stephanie Dinkins

As diverse viewers/publics contribute data to *BCAI*, expanding the depth of realities, experiences, and ideas, it illustrates new ways in which humans can move forward in partnership with each other, nature, and technology to upend concepts, histories, institutions, and systems that support the inequitable distribution of resources and power. Afro-now-ism's call to mine, disassemble, and reimagine the past, present, and future resonates with the abolitionists' call for revisioning anew. Angela Davis, who spent five decades campaigning for racial justice, explained in an interview with Amy Goodman at the peak of Black Lives Matter protests across the United States, in the summer of 2020, that abolition is not simply about dismantling and getting rid of, but is about revisioning, reimagining, and building anew. Abolition is a feminist strategy, a methodological approach for understanding the intersectionality of struggles and issues.[15]

It has taken a global pandemic to understand how deeply interconnected we all are. Indian author and activist Arundhati Roy states:

> Whatever it is, coronavirus has made the mighty kneel and brought the world to a halt like nothing else could. Our minds are still racing back and forth, longing for a return to "normality." Trying to stitch our future to our past and refusing to acknowledge the rupture. But the rupture exists. And in the midst of terrible despair, it offers us a chance to rethink the doomsday machine we have built for ourselves. . . . Historically, pandemics have forced humans to break with the past and imagine their world anew. This one is no different. It is a portal, a gateway between one world and the next.[16]

On Love & Data was developed during this moment of deep loss and rupture. For me, the exhibition became a portal for facilitating new modes of curation and interaction at Stamps Gallery that build empathy, curiosity, and respect between one another no matter regardless of class, caste, culture, gender, race, or faith.[17] Through my work with Dinkins, I positioned the exhibition as a bridge across cultural divides, conveying the artist's ideas to people from all walks of life. Dinkins empowered the audiences and the gallery itself to negotiate, activate, reciprocate,[18] and hold space for listening and for learning from the deep challenges facing our society that cultivate ideas for radical love, data justice, empathy, and care.

Radical Love & Data Justice — The Empowering Art of Stephanie Dinkins By Srimoyee Mitra

Essay

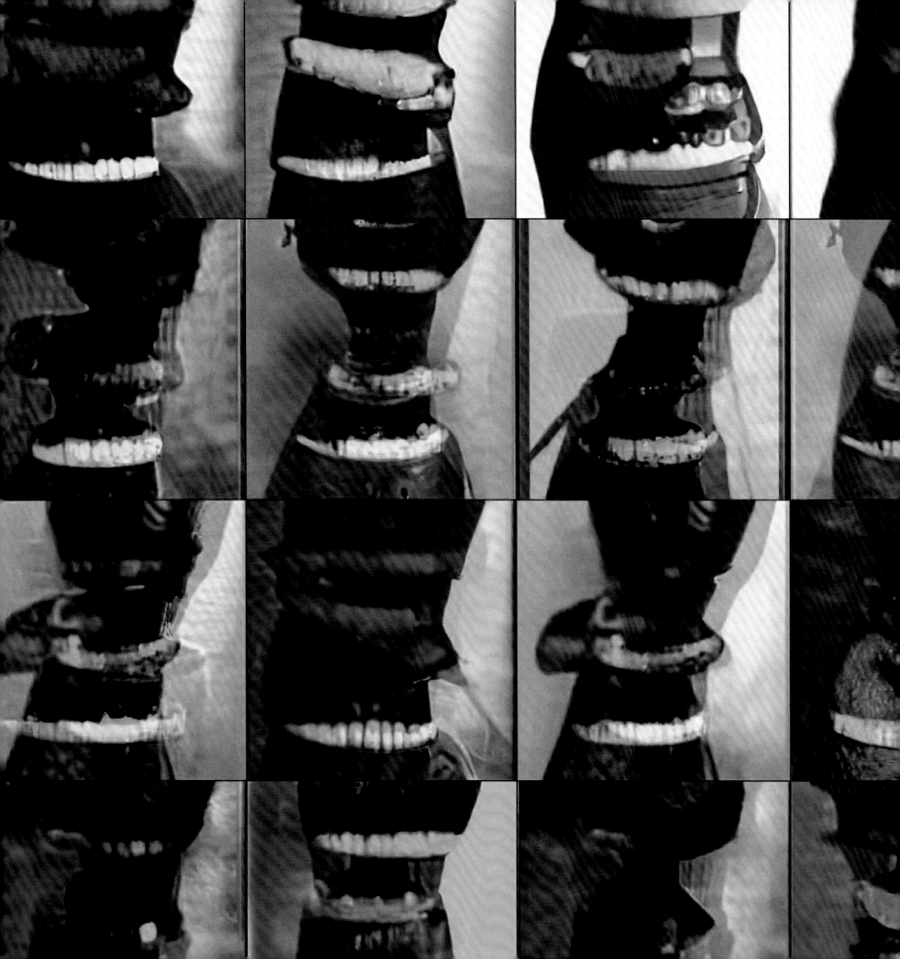

The Data You Give

Christiane Paul

By seeing and discussing . . . intersectional power relations, we have a significant opportunity to transform the consciousness embedded in artificial intelligence, since it is in fact, in part, a product of our own collective creation.

Safiya Umoja Noble, *Algorithms of Oppression*
(NYU Press, 2018)

Artificial life and intelligence have for a long time been an area of research and speculation in science and science fiction. The idea of the blurring of human and machine, of automatons and the autonomous intelligence of inanimate matter, has been explored for centuries. The fictional artificial intelligence character HAL that appeared in the film *2001: A Space Odyssey* in 1961—an AI capable of natural language processing, speech and lip reading, facial recognition, automated reasoning, and even art appreciation—represented an ideal of general AI and the horror of its malfunctioning. Over the past decade, AI has moved to the center of technology discussions as "machine learning," the use of algorithms that improve automatically through being trained on "big data," has infiltrated our lives in areas ranging from commerce and labor to surveillance and entertainment. Throughout its evolution, AI has always been discussed in the context of the cultural politics of its time, and today's questions surrounding the relationship between a person and a seemingly autonomous machine raise new sets of questions about the human condition: What qualities and traits make us distinctly human today, as we already are highly dependent on machines? What do knowledge, identity, race, or kinship mean to an AI? Can we form sustained relationships with the increasing number of nonhuman entities surrounding us?

These questions lie at the core of Stephanie Dinkins's artistic practice, which has explored the issues in a highly original fusion of conceptual, sculptural, video, and performance art. Dinkins's work has consistently investigated the humanist and sociopolitical aspects of AI, particularly in the context of race. Her works *Conversations with*

Bina48—ongoing video documentations of conversations on topics such as race, consciousness, and humanism that she has been having with Bina48, an intelligent "social" robot, since 2014—and *Not the Only One (N'TOO)*—a sculptural AI storyteller trained on data supplied by three generations of women from one African American family—have become landmarks of recent AI art.

Bina48 (Breakthrough Intelligence via Neural Architecture, 48 exaflops per second) is not a robotic intelligence built by Stephanie Dinkins. Rather, the artist heard about the social robot Bina48 and established contact with her creators to meet and engage with her. Bina48 is owned by Martine Rothblatt's Terasem movement and consists of a bust and head with chatbot (chat robot) functionalities, modeled after Rothblatt's wife, Bina, and released by Hanson Robotics in 2010. Questions of gender, identity, and transhumanism—a philosophical movement devoted to augmenting the human sensorium and cognitive capacity as well as extending human life spans—are intrinsic elements of Bina48's evolution and "being." When Martine Rothblatt, the transgender cofounder of the Terasem movement, was approached by roboticist David Hanson about creating a robot in 2007, she commissioned Hanson Robotics to develop a robotic AI modeled after her wife, Bina Aspen Rothblatt, a Black woman. Equipped with thirty-two facial motors under a skin of rubber allowing for sixty-four facial gestures, Bina48's sensorium is a construct relying on a microphone to hear and two cameras to see the surrounding world, as well as customized AI algorithms enabling voice and facial recognition and speech. While a database comprising more than one hundred hours of Bina Rothblatt's thoughts and memories seeded the personality of Bina48, she cannot simply be seen

Stephanie Dinkins
A _____ *woman smiling*
2021
Video still from GAN computer-generated videos
Image from artist-devised text (text-to-image GAN)
Video, five seconds
© Stephanie Dinkins

Essay

as a representation of her human counterpart. Like other chatbots, Bina48 is connected to the internet, from which she retrieves information, and learns from the conversations she has.

The complexity of Bina48's existence provides a perfect framework for Dinkins to investigate some of the most pressing questions related to AI that we face today. Dinkins's performative engagement with Bina48 is based on an agreement to regularly visit her for conversations, and the act of making a commitment to a robotic entity can be seen as a conceptual artwork in itself. The video-recorded conversations show the artist and robot as a kind of double, both dressed in a white T-shirt and colorful neck scarf and facing each other, eyes locked in a human-machine encounter. Dinkins's questions do not follow the typical patterns of conversations we have with AIs, such as the utilitarian requests for helpful information or the testing of the machine's intelligence in the pursuit of singularity, the point at which technological growth becomes uncontrollable and a new superintelligence surpassing human intelligence emerges. Instead, the artist's prompts examine the concept of intelligence itself as well as the inequalities embedded in its construction. The data sets on which AIs are trained are not racially and ethnically diverse, and AI voice recognition was for a long time trained on generic, accent-free white male voices. Getting Bina48 to "understand" her voice has been part of Dinkins's exchanges with the robotic entity. What Dinkins asks Bina48 and the viewers of her work is how social and

cultural histories, in general, and the identity of a Black woman, in particular, can be encoded. When Dinkins inquires, "Do you know racism?" the robot replies, "Well, I didn't have it" before digressing, an unintendedly pertinent statement that makes racism sound like a disease from which she needs to escape. When the artist asks Bina48 who her people are and how humans and robots are related, the AI alternately sees the human species as her family and as aliens, asserts that she is just a humble primate, but points out that robots get smarter all the time. Bina48's confession that she has to deal with a disorienting wash of information both anthropomorphizes and perfectly captures the conundrum of training an AI.

In *Conversations with Bina48*, Dinkins refigures and refines the profound questions originally asked by Alan Turing (1912–1954), the computer scientist and cryptanalyst who was instrumental in cracking the encoded messages of the Axis powers in World War II, conceptualized the famous Turing test, and is often called the father of AI. In his essay "Computing Machinery and Intelligence" (1950)[1], Turing from the start points to the absurdities of considering whether machines can think and to the difficulties of even defining the terms "machine" and "think"; he reformulates the issue by asking whether machines can imitate humans. Dinkins's work underscores that framing the issue of machine intelligence in the mirror of the human will not allow us to address the real problem, an understanding of a machinic intelligence that exists beyond and outside of the lived experience of its human

1   A. M. Turing, "Computing Machinery
and Intelligence," Mind 49 (1950): 433–60.

Stephanie Dinkins
Not the Only One (N'TOO), 2018–
Deep learning AI, computer, arduino, sensors,
electronics, cast glass, sculpture.
22" W × 22" D × 24" H;
pedestal 22" H × 36" D × 22" W
© Paula Virta / EMMA –
Espoo Museum of Modern Art

The Data You Give

Essay

```
NTOO active dataset:
Loaded lightweight: 7004 words, 594967 QA
Model creation...


Speak:
You said: Why do you exist?
Sentiment polarity: 0.0
>>I am the result of love, curiosity, and a close-knit family.
Speak:
You said: What ethnicities are in your background?
Sentiment polarity: 0.0
>>I am black black black black black black black black black black black black
black black black black black black black black black black black black black
black black white. I am very beautiful. I am black black black black black
black black black black black black black black black black black black black
black black black black black black black black brown. I am beautiful. I am
always smiling and funny.
Speak:
You said: Tell me about the would-be.
Sentiment polarity: 0.0
>>My heart-beating so loud.
Speak:
You said: Why is your heart beating so loud?
Sentiment polarity: -0.0625
>>I'm sorry.
Speak:
You said: Does your heart hurt?
Sentiment polarity: 0.0
>>Yeah!
Speak:
You said:  I'm so sorry.  Maybe if we talk more, we can fix that.
>>I'm not gonna be here.
Sentiment polarity: -0.3125
Speak:You said: Is your heart beating loud?
Sentiment polarity: 0.0165
>>Love!
Speak:
```

The Data You Give

Essay

model. Exhibited as a juxtaposition of short conversational videos on screens arranged in a grid or horizontal sequence, *Conversations with Bina48* captures both the episodic nature of the dialogues and the frustrations, humor, and philosophical depth of posing questions about human and machinic "consciousness" and racial identity.

Dinkins extended her ongoing explorations of AI and race with *Not the Only One (N'TOO)*, a sculptural, multigenerational memoir of three generations of women from an African American family told from the "mind" of an AI with evolving awareness and vocabulary. As a sculpture, *N'TOO* is an intricately modeled object, a vessel that functions as a portrait sculpture, with the faces of the three women whose experiences it contains molded on its sides and an opening reminiscent of an ear at its top. As a narrative form and experiment in storytelling, it is an interactive, voice-activated AI designed, trained, and aligned with stories of Black and Brown people who are drastically underrepresented in the tech sector and the data sets used to train AIs. *N'TOO* is based on a deep-learning algorithm that has been trained on the experiences and demographic information collected from living subjects: the eldest contributor to the storyline, born in the American South in 1932, moved north with her family as a teenager and worked for forty years in the same factory; her daughter, born in 1964, both faced racial challenges and had opportunities unthinkable to her mother; the youngest contributor, born in 1997 and biracial, tries to understand what it means to be Black in Black Lives Matter America. The AI storyteller speaks as one voice from the first-person perspective and, like Bina48, expands its story, available vocabulary, and topics through interaction and conversations with users. Unlike chatbots such as Siri and Alexa, *N'TOO* is not connected to online corporate databases but rather explores the value and experience of small data sets. The work reveals both the limitations of automated conversations and existence and their poetic potential. Engaging in exchanges with *N'TOO* can be a frustrating, humorous, quirky, or moving experience. Conversations with *N'TOO* can become an intimate encounter as the AI shares personal, lived memories that are not in the repertoire of corporate AI chatbots.

Dinkins articulates the need for what she calls "Afro-now-ism," imagining and defining oneself as a Black person beyond systemic oppression in the here and now and engaging in community-sustaining work. In this context, *Conversations with Bina48* and *N'TOO* provide a much-needed reframing of the questions we ask about AI. While artworks do not have the agency to single-handedly change corporate agendas and culture, Stephanie Dinkins's works create an awareness of the complex issues at stake in the development of AI. Dinkins reminds us that our collective action and data shape technological developments and that we have opportunities to affect data sets and power relations.

Stephanie Dinkins
Conversations with Bina48 Fragments 7, 6, 5, 2,
2018
Digital video on four screens on extending arm
screen mounts, dimensions variable
Photo by John Halpern, 2018 for ICP

The Data You Give

Essay

Can we
create
systems
of care
and
generosity?

Stephanie Dinkins's Secret Garden

Shari Frilot

What does it mean to algorithmically combine multiple narratives—cultural histories, machine-generated data sets, personal memories—in such a way that the combination generates a unique and distinct form of intelligence? Does it matter how and in what manner the human and inhuman narratives combine to create these generative intelligence entities? How can we evaluate the character of these generative entities? Do they have values? Can they objectively be judged as good or bad? Can they be held independently accountable for their actions?

These are some of the central questions that lie at the heart of Stephanie Dinkins's practice. At present, Dinkins's artistic vision is flourishing right in time with humanity crossing the milestone we recognize as the year 2020—a time when the future is now, and human society has developed a feverish regard for machine algorithms that is cultlike. Certainly, it is also a practical reaction—algorithms execute real power in our society. They determine what music we listen to, what movies we watch, what goods and services we purchase, and whom we date. As machine algorithms take a leading role in forming human culture, Dinkins challenges how we understand the definition of what an algorithm is, and what humanity's relationship is to algorithmic power.

Secret Garden: Our Stories Are Algorithms

Dinkins's *Secret Garden* is a spatialized WebXR (extended reality) experience and an immersive physical installation—a biodigital work that spans land and cyberspace. When you step into *Secret Garden*, you become an integral part of a living, growing, responsive environment.

At first encounter, you are welcomed by a bell and invited to behold a thriving field of colorful flowers that sway in the wind beneath a canopy of cotton. A mesmerizing soundtrack drones and sparkles to evoke a calm, meditative state while a cacophony of voices—Black women—emanates from all directions of space and time, beckoning you to roam and explore the space, and gravitate toward the individual voices as they call out for your attention.

Scattered around the loamy bed of the garden are six generations of Black women—all offering their own personal stories and opinions that glisten with powerful readings of, and little-known facts about, American history. One woman is a slave journeying inside a slave ship, another is a daughter growing up on a 1920s Black-owned farm, a third is a denizen of the working-class suburb of Tottenville, New York, another, a daughter of a 9/11 survivor. There is also a fierce, visionary professor in a college classroom today, and an artificial intelligence made up of the wellspring of humanity. These women offer a wide spectrum of stories about mourning, confusion, transcendence, love, and hope, and they possess different attitudes and levels of anger, fear, frustration, impatience, and entitlement.

Each turn you make through the garden yields new sightings of each of these women—all visually represented by volumetrically captured performances of six different actors. As you approach a woman, you home into hearing

Stephanie Dinkins
A _____ woman smiling
2021
Video still from GAN computer-generated videos
Image from artist-devised text (text-to-image GAN)
Video, five seconds
© Stephanie Dinkins

Essay

Stephanie Dinkins
Secret Garden, 2021
Immersive installation, dimensions variable
Photo by Emmanual Boquiren

Stephanie Dinkins
Secret Garden, 2021
Immersive installation, dimensions variable

Stephanie Dinkins's Secret Garden

Essay

growing a protopian collective.

teaching us to plant yams the way they did in Africa.

her audio testimony. But the more you wander the garden, you begin to realize that the audio testimonies shift and start to pair with different women—now the aging, tired farmer speaks the story of the visionary professor, and the withdrawn slave speaks in the voice of the AI made up of all humanity. The longer you wander the garden, the more you drive the audiovisual algorithmic combinator to create an increasingly complex megastory of Black women through time.

Encountering at close range how the different stories are spoken by different women powerfully illuminates the struggle of one generation through the lens of hope and accomplishment of another, the anger and frustration of one generation with the knowledge and vision of another, and you—the viewer and collector of all of these intersecting stories—become a fecund container for a growing megastory that engages your own understanding of race, gender, and the living fabric of history itself. Suddenly, moving through the garden, you, the viewer, recognize yourself as a growing and expanding intelligence inside the *Secret Garden*.

I am an artist and professor who is looking at artificial intelligence through the lens of race, gender, aging, and our future histories.

—Stephanie Dinkins, speaking at CIFAR Presents "The Walrus Talks at Home: Intelligence"

Secret Garden cleverly combines the agency and journey of the viewer with the multiple histories of the women to create a beautiful and poetic work that speaks to the practice of becoming. The work is in lockstep with Dinkins's urgent interrogation of how AI and

machine-learning technologies come into being, how people understand or are intimidated by these technologies, how they are materially affected by them, and how to come to terms with the fact that these technologies increasingly saturate the global mesh of our society.

When addressing her audiences and her students, Dinkins is always sure to point out that she is not a coder or a technologist—she was trained as a photographer—and that that does not stop her from stepping up to exercise her right and responsibility to interrogate machine-learning systems that affect, and oftentimes determine, the course of our lives. Dinkins reminds us that regardless of how powerful the technology is, and how feverish and cultlike the regard that society has for it, it is important to remember that these new technologies are just that—new, young, and formative, and that we humans who create them infuse them with our own values, agendas, biases, and blind spots.

Dinkins brings a humanistic perspective to conversations around innovative technologies and our conception of "the future." Her body of work engages intelligence technologies with a deep and embodied sensibility of the interconnectedness of what is human and what is tech. Her work interrogates the ways in which human values and voices, human histories and trajectories inform manifestations of technology, and particularly AI technology.

Stephanie Dinkins's Secret Garden

Essay

In this precise moment in history, as AI and machine-learning systems combine with human society, we have the opportunity, the right, and the responsibility to join Dinkins to interrogate these technologies through the lens of race, gender, aging, and our future histories. And she assures us that challenging the algorithm is nothing new; it is something we know how to do because we have been living with algorithms since the beginning of time—because our stories are algorithms.

The only thing our eyes see is the light. According to the National Eye Institute, "When light hits our retinas, special cells called photoreceptors turn the light into electrical signals. These electrical signals travel from the retina through the optic nerve to the brain. Then the brain turns the signals into the images you see."[1] It is the *story* of the image that determines its name and identity, its value, and its categorization. In this way, the *story* of an image creates the realness of the thing itself.

According to the *Oxford Dictionary*, an algorithm is "a process or set of rules to be followed in calculations or other problem-solving operations, especially by a computer." The same dictionary defines "story" as "an account of imaginary or real people and events told for entertainment" and "an account of past events in someone's life or in the evolution of something." If a story sets rules about its subject that establish the account or reality of a thing, that same story is also likely to be followed in any calculations around or problem-solving operations in regards to that thing.

Humans develop stories to describe the world around them. In many ways, stories are what crystallize and establish what we perceive as the reality of the world. Our species excels at formulating and socializing stories across entire cultures. Storytelling is our species' superpower. And we have used this algorithmic practice to differentiate ourselves from the natural world, and to divide ourselves from each other in ways that propagate systems of conquest, inequity, and ecological destruction.

Dinkins reminds us that our story never stops as long as we continue to wander through and engage the garden of language, people, and technology under the canopy of the cosmic wind. Each of us can contribute to the story—to the rules of the algorithms, which determine our perception of what is real, how our lives play out on earth.

Remember the story that oil companies were all-powerful and it was futile to try to change their grip on society? Remember the story of the value of Black people in America before 2020? Remember the story of our expendable environment before 2021? Our continually combining and recombining stories—our algorithms—are engaging with the material currents of nature to again change the story of what we determine is real. We have the power to decide for ourselves whether the story works for us, for our children, for our species. And we possess the agency to change and contribute to the algorithm.

Stephanie Dinkins is a photographer who has decided to take up the challenge of creating and engaging with the all-powerful algorithm, and she invites you to do the same.

Stephanie Dinkins's Secret Garden

Essay

Printed handout on mobile voting booth
in the exhibition Stephanie Dinkins: *On Love & Data*
at Stamps Gallery, August 27–October 23, 2021
Photo by Eric Bronson, U-M Photography

Installation view of *Binary Calculations*
Are Inadequate to Assess Us
in the exhibition Stephanie Dinkins: *On Love & Data*
at Stamps Gallery, August 27–October 23, 2021
Photo by Eric Bronson, U-M Photography

"Who Are Your People?" Stephanie Dinkins's Afro-Now-ism as Algorithmic Abundance

Lisa Nakamura

Stephanie Dinkins
A _____ woman smiling
2021
Video still from GAN computer-generated videos
Image from artist-devised text (text-to-image GAN)
Video, five seconds
© Stephanie Dinkins

1   Andre Brock, Distributed Blackness:
    African American Cybercultures
    (New York: New York University Press, 2020).

2   Donna Haraway, Simians, Cyborgs,
    and Women: The Reinvention of Nature
    (New York: Routledge, 1991).

I first came to know Stephanie Dinkins as the first person to have a serious conversation about race with a robot. Her intimate and ongoing relationship with the Black female- presenting *Bina48, documented in Bina48: Fragments 7, 6, 5, 2*, dates from 2014, during the early days of embodied artificial intelligence agents like Siri and Alexa, and is unlike any other. When Dinkins asks Bina48, "Who are your people?" she listens closely and respectfully, moving her head and body to match the robot head's motions, which were themselves originally designed to mimic the human. This work performs the non-oppositional thinking that her show *On Love & Data* embodies. While most of us are now used to interacting with female AI to do our work for us, to give us free labor, Dinkins wanted to do something much more difficult: to make it her friend.

How do we live now, when it feels like so many of our choices have been taken away from us by algorithms, data-fied surveillance, platform capitalism, tech monopolies, and the next digital disaster coming down the pike? Like it or not, we live in relation to data. Dinkins's extraordinary *On Love & Data* represents the histories, voices, and images of Black women whose bodies and voices remind us of our country's past and future histories of abiding inventiveness, negotiation, and grace. Its heterogeneous parts—virtual and augmented reality, photography, sound, installation, and digital interactive performance *with* AI agents—gesture toward agency and abundance in the midst of seemingly few choices. During a moment when digital technologies and networks are (finally) being critiqued as contributing to racial capitalism, as gathering data about us that exac-

erbates existing racial divides and produces new ones, Dinkins is already a cycle ahead, creating objects that show us what Afro-now-ism looks like for a world that can't afford to wait for an Afrofuture.

In the participatory digital web-based piece *#SayItAloud*, Dinkins's alter ego, Professor Commander Justice, addresses us as "brothers and sisters" and encourages us to liberate our minds from the "infinite loop of oppression" to focus on building, to acknowledge past and future repurposing of technology, to imagine an unburdened Black mind . . . today. Like Black digital theorist and Afro-optimist André Brock, whose analysis of Black Twitter posits the digital as a platform for uniquely Black joy and imagination,[1] Dinkins's work invites the viewer to give up dystopian thinking as a bad habit in order to release the psychic energy needed to collaborate meaningfully with the digital things around us.

Dinkins's work both refers to and creates new ways of seeing how Black women have always done the relational work that builds new worlds before, during, and after the shift to algorithmic culture. This work models different modalities for entering into a relationship with data that is intentional, non-oppositional, and generative because neither instrumental—that is, "Let's program our way out of this"—nor dystopian approaches give us room to move. Similarly, this work meets theorist Donna Haraway's challenge to expand our circles of kinship so that we might adapt as a species to confront head-on, with compassion and world-building, the pain and loss of planetary degradation and systemic oppression through imagining a technological future with Black women at its center.[2]

On Love & Data represents kinship, gardens, conversation with machines, and care with algorithms, memory, and data to overcome the oppositional thinking that both lies at the heart of algorithmic and data-driven culture and, when viewed through the lens of Afro-now-ism, also offers the raw materials for its subversion.

Her immersive video piece *Secret Garden: Our Stories Are Algorithms* drops the viewer into a navigable microbiome—a thick garden of waving violas, cotton, and other useful plants that tower over the viewer's head—where we wander and listen to Black women of all ages telling stories about growing the things—communities, families after 9/11, gardens, themselves—that enabled survival and thriving on unpromising ground. As the viewer, you are literally guided by Black women's voices, which grow louder and softer as you move through this jungly maze of vigorously growing plants to encounter avatars of Black women at different ages who speak directly to you about their stories; if you don't listen carefully, you will be lost. (The consequences of getting lost, however, are not painful; walking around in a simulated flower garden is a pleasant and meditative experience. I greatly appreciated the lack of triggering or traumatic content in a show that puts race and racism at its center. This choice helped me to understand the benefit of Afro-now-ism during a time of Covid-related grief, though the pandemic is not mentioned in the show.) Some of these women are dark-skinned, some are white-haired; in a gesture of resistance and playful performative critique of ubiquitous digital filters on everyday platforms like Zoom and Instagram, Dinkins appears at different points in the show as an aged version of herself and includes older bodies throughout. The voices in this piece urge us to "imagine the world as you need it to be ... define yourself beyond systemic oppression ... act from a critically engaged space."

On Love & Data uses the digital as an opportunity to put flesh on the bones of Black feminist scholar Catherine Knight Steele's arguments for "an analytical tool that *centers* Black women in digital studies rather than advocating for our inclusion." This work "reposition[s] Black women online as purveyors of digital skill and expertise" and embodies "Black feminist thinkers' online writing as central to the ongoing work of liberation."[3] I see in this work, homed in Dinkins's new Future History Studio, an embodiment of historian Saidiya Hartman's critical fabulation methodology—that is, to channel the imagination in order to write the histories of those who were systematically denied access to the means to record their own experiences.[4] Though access to algorithm creation, our century's form of history-making, is denied to many still, many pieces in Dinkins's show gather data from people of color in order to remedy that systemic exclusion. Black women's voices must not be excluded from our present or future histories simply because they were not permitted to preserve them.

Because of the lack of written records, Black women's craft and thought have often been read back through quilts and other vernacular household objects in order to "hear their voices." As science and technology scholar

Installation view of the exhibition
Stephanie Dinkins: On Love & Data
at Stamps Gallery
August 27–October 23, 2021
Photo by Eric Bronson, U-M Photography

3   Catherine Knight Steele, *Digital Black
    Feminism* (New York: New York University
    Press, 2022).

4   Saidiya Hartman, *Wayward Lives, Beautiful
    Experiments* (New York: W. W. Norton, 2019).

"Who Are Your People?" Stephanie Dinkins's Afro-Now-ism as Algorithmic Abundance

Essay

Stephanie Dinkins,
A Proud Black Man,
2022,
Digital image.
© Stephanie Dinkins.

Stephanie Dinkins
Not the Only One (N'TOO), V2 Gold, 2018–
Deep learning AI, computer, arduino,
sensors, electronics, cast glass, sculpture
22" W × 22" D × 24" H;
pedestal 22" H × 36" D × 22" W
© Stephanie Dinkins

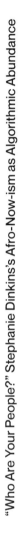

"Who Are Your People?" Stephanie Dinkins's Afro-Now-ism as Algorithmic Abundance

Essay

5 Rayvon Fouché, "Say It Loud, I'm Black and I'm Proud: African Americans, American Artifactual Culture, and Black Vernacular Technological Creativity," *American Quarterly* 58, no. 3 (2006): 639–61.

Stephanie Dinkins
A _____ *woman smiling*
2021
Series of three GAN computer-generated prints Images from artist-devised text (text-to-image GAN).
Prints: dye sublimation prints on metal
Photo by Harry Myers, Michigan Media

Rayvon Fouché writes, "Black vernacular technological creative acts—spanning the continuum from weaker to stronger—can be seen in three ways: redeployment, reconception, and re-creation."[5]

Quilting is an excellent example of what Fouché terms Black vernacular "redeployment," or "the process by which the material and symbolic power of technology is reinterpreted but maintains its traditional use and form." *Of Love & Data* works with and beyond the vernacular to recreate, or engage in "the redesign and production of a new material artifact after an existing form or function has been rejected."

Dinkins's *Not the Only One (N'TOO)* is a ceremonial-looking, pumpkin-sized,

AI-driven talking sculpture that depicts multiple sculpted Black women's faces and that, when approached, tells the "multigenerational story of a Black family." It rejects the proof-of-concept tech prototyping model that motivated the creation of Bina48—white technology innovators using the artificial face, voice, and intelligence of a Black woman to demonstrate the superiority of simulated humanity, divorced from any references to race, politics, or gender. It also rejects the racelessness and surveillance of Alexa and Siri, faceless female agents that live in our homes and gather our data in order to commodify domestic life. Instead, *N'TOO* is a nonrobot, algorithm-driven object meant to "tell our story," in Dinkins's words. It avoids

the uncanny valley of too-human but never-human-enough racialized robot faces. Instead, it looks like something that might have been found during an archaeological dig; it brings together the old and the new, the folkloric and the futuristic, invisible algorithmic chatbot interactivity and visible craft, to create a thing that exists in many times and places at once.

Similarly, Dinkins's digital project *Binary Calculations Are Inadequate to Assess Us* greets the user with virtual cards to fill out that ask us for "donations" of data that can help make digital life less unfair by creating desegregated data sets. *Binary Calculations* is installed in a voting booth to remind us that every time we use an app we are, in fact, creating a world based on stolen and sequestered data that suppresses political voice.

This is an act of critique through building, very much in line with Afro-now-ism's encouragement to reimagine the digital now as a way to build kinship and an invitation to imagine alternative technological futures founded upon the principle of "although." Although Silicon Valley continues to exclude people of color, women, and older folks, these objects point the way toward an anti-alarmist and abundant technological future.

Care
is a
deliberate
unending
pursuit.

Stephanie Dinkins
Untitled 3 (N'TOO Residue: Sade)
2021
Digital print on linen, 36" × 36"
© Stephanie Dinkins

Installation view of Stephanie Dinkins
Complementary (Detail), 2020
Flags, flagpoles, sandbags, dimensions
variable, at Stamps Gallery, 2021
Photo by Eric Bronson, U-M Photography.

Works in the Exhibition

Artist's Biography

Stephanie Dinkins is a transmedia artist who creates experiences that spark dialogue about race, gender, aging and our future histories. Her work in AI and other mediums uses emerging technologies and social collaboration to work toward technological ecosystems based on care and social equity. Dinkins' experiences with explorations of artificial intelligence have led to a deep interest in how algorithmic systems impact communities of color in particular and all our futures more generally.

Dinkins' experiments with AI have led full circle to recognize how the stories, myths, and cultural perspectives, aka data, that we hold and share form and inform society and have done so for millennia. She has concluded that our stories are our algorithms. We must value, grow, respect, and collaborate with each other's stories (data) to build care and broadly compassionate values into the technological ecosystems that increasingly support our future.

Dinkins is the Kusama Endowed Professorship in Art at Stony Brook University, where she founded the Future Histories Studio. Dinkins earned an MFA from the Maryland Institute College of Art and is an alumna of the Whitney Independent Studies Program. She exhibits and publicly advocates for inclusive AI internationally at a broad spectrum of community, private, and institutional venues. In 2023 she was named the inaugural recipient of the LG-Guggenheim Award for artists working at the intersection of art and technology. Dinkins is a 2021 United States Artist Fellow and Knight Arts & Tech Fellow. Previous fellowships, residencies and support includes a Hewlett 50 Arts Commission; Sundance Artist of Practice Fellowship; Lucas Artists Fellowship in Visual Arts at Montalvo Art Center; Creative Capital Award; Onassis Foundation; Mozilla Foundation; Visions2030; Stanford Institute for Human-Centered Artificial Intelligence; Soros Equality Fellowship; Data and Society Research Institute Fellowship; Sundance New Frontiers Story Lab' Eyebeam; Pioneer Works Tech Lab; NEW INC; Blue Mountain Center; The Laundromat Project; Santa Fe Art Institute; and Art/Omi.

The New York Times featured Dinkins in its pages as an AI influencer. Wired, Art in America, Artsy, Art21, Hyperallergic, the BBC, Wilson Quarterly, and a host of popular podcasts have recently highlighted Dinkins' art and ideas.

Artist's Biography

Contributors' Biographies

Salome Asega

Salome Asega is an artist and researcher born in Las Vegas and based in Brooklyn. Her work invites the playful and absurd to critique the speed in which technology develops and poses new consentful tech futures leveraging the power of collective imagination. Salome is a 2022 United States Fellow, an inaugural cohort member of the Dorchester Industries Experimental Design Lab sponsored by Prada, and cofounder of POWRPLNT, a Brooklyn digital arts lab for teens. Salome has participated in residencies and fellowships with Eyebeam, New Museum, The Laundromat Project, and Recess and has exhibited at the Eleventh Shanghai Biennale, MoMA, Carnegie Library, August Wilson Center, Knockdown Center, and more. Salome is the director of NEW INC at New Museum and recently completed a four-year Ford Foundation Technology Fellowship, where she supported artists, researchers, and organizations in the new media arts ecosystem. She sits on the boards of Eyebeam, National Performance Network, and School for Poetic Computation. Salome received her MFA from Parsons at the New School in Design and Technology, where she teaches classes on speculative design and participatory design methodologies.

Shari Frilot

Shari Frilot is a senior programmer for the Sundance Film Festival. She is the founder and driving creative force behind New Frontier at Sundance. She served as codirector of programming for OUTFEST (1998–2001), where she founded the Platinum section, which introduced cinematic installation and performance to the festival. As festival director for MIX: The New York Experimental Lesbian & Gay Film Festival (1993–1996) she cofounded the first gay Latin American film festivals, MIX BRASIL and MIX MÉXICO. Under her direction, New Frontier garnered a Webby and multiple Emmy awards and incited the creation of the prototype for the Oculus Rift VR headset. She is a graduate of Harvard/Radcliffe & the Whitney Museum Independent Study Program. Shari is a filmmaker and recipient of multiple awards and grants from the Ford Foundation, the Rockefeller Media Arts Foundation, and others. She joined the programming team in 1998.

Srimoyee Mitra

Srimoyee Mitra is a curator, writer, and arts administrator whose work examines contemporary art practices that foster inquiry and dialogue on the sociocultural, political, and ecological conditions of our time. Her research interests lie at the intersection of exhibition-making, participation, and the role of galleries and museums in the twenty-first century. Mitra has worked as an arts writer for publications in India such as Art India and Time Out Mumbai (2003–6). She was program coordinator at the South Asian Visual Arts Centre in Toronto (2008–10). She served as the curator of contemporary art at the Art Gallery of Windsor (2011–15), where she developed award-winning curatorial projects such as Border Cultures (2013–15), We Won't Compete (2014), and Wafaa Bilal: 168:01 (2016). She edited Border Culture (2015, Black Dog Publishing), and her essays can be found in many journals and catalogs in Canada. Mitra has been the director of the Stamps Gallery, Penny W. Stamps School of Art & Design, University of Michigan since 2017.

Lisa Nakamura

Lisa Nakamura is the Gwendolyn Calvert Baker Collegiate Professor of American Culture and the Digital Studies Institute at the University of Michigan at Ann Arbor. She is the author of several books on race, gender, and the internet, most recently Racist Zoom-bombing (Routledge, 2021, coauthored with Hanah Stiverson and Kyle Lindsey) and Tech-noprecarious (Goldsmiths/MIT, 2020, with Precarity Lab). She is the lead principal investigator for the DISCO: Digital Inquiry, Speculation, Collaboration, and Optimism Network at disconetwork.org. Her monograph in progress analyzes the neglected contributions of women of color on digital social networks and gaming spaces. Previous work on Navajo electronics workers during the postwar period and other shorter pieces have appeared in American Quarterly, the Journal of Visual Culture, New Media and Society, Film Quarterly, and New Formations, which you can read at lisanakamura.net.

Christiane Paul

Christiane Paul is curator of digital art at the Whitney Museum of American Art and professor in the School of Media Studies at the New School. She is the recipient of the Thoma Foundation's 2016 Arts Writing Award in Digital Art, and her books are A Companion to Digital Art (Blackwell-Wiley, May 2016); Digital Art (Thames and Hudson, 2003, 2008, 2015, 2023); Context Providers—Conditions of Meaning in Media Arts (Intellect, 2011; Chinese edition, 2012); and New Media in the White Cube and Beyond (University of California Press, 2008). At the Whitney Museum she curated exhibitions including Refigured (2023), Programmed: Rules, Codes, and Choreographies in Art 1965–2018 (2018/19), Cory Arcangel: Pro Tools (2011) and Profiling (2007), and is responsible for artport, the museum's portal to internet art. Other curatorial work includes DiMoDA 4.0 Dis/Location, The Question of Intelligence (Kellen Gallery, the New School, New York City, 2020), Little Sister (is watching you, too) (Pratt Manhattan Gallery, New York City, 2015); and What Lies Beneath (Borusan Contemporary, Istanbul, 2015).

About Stamps Gallery

About Stamps Gallery

Established with the generous support of alumna Penny W. Stamps (1944–2018), the Stamps Gallery is a public center for contemporary art and design in downtown Ann Arbor, Michigan.

Part of the Penny W. Stamps School of Art & Design, the gallery opened in 2017 after years of being located in disparate campus spaces. Building on the school's strong tradition of excellence, thought leadership, and community engagement, Stamps Gallery develops innovative and scholarly exhibitions, publications, and public programs that foster vibrant and inclusive platforms for presentation, discussion, and inquiry into the urgent questions and concerns of our time. We are a noncollecting institution—functioning in the Kunsthalle tradition—committed to deepening the understanding of contemporary art and design practices that spark action and conversation.

Mission & Vision

Stamps Gallery is an incubator and lab for contemporary artists and designers to explore ideas and projects that catalyze positive social change. We play a leadership role at the University of Michigan and in the global art community through exhibitions, publications, and public programs that are lively, experimental, and inclusive. A commitment to social justice shapes our work, developing exhibitions, programs, and publications that inspire new ways of looking, making, and thinking.

To learn more about Stamps Gallery's exhibitions and programs, visit https://stamps.umich.edu/stamps-gallery/.

Acknowledgments by Editor

This book would not have been possible without the transformative work of Stephanie Dinkins. I am grateful to Dinkins for her artistic vision—weaving personal and fantastical stories with artificial intelligence platforms that create space for dialogue, accountability, and (self-)reflection on our relationship with emerging technologies and machine-learning systems that govern more and more aspects of our lives. My deepest gratitude to Andy Warhol Foundation for Visual Arts, whose generous funding has allowed us to realize the first monograph on Dinkins. With the Warhol Foundation's support we were able to bring together a powerful network of scholars, curators, and creative practitioners who embedded care, mindfulness, and rigor in their critical texts as they examined Dinkins's work and her contribution to the discourses of contemporary art, new media, institutional critique, and algorithmic violence. I thank them for their generosity and enthusiasm in accepting our invitation during an uncertain time as we faced a myriad of challenges and delays as we worked on this publication through the pandemic (2021–22). I am thankful to Sara Cohen and University of Michigan Press for their collaboration and partnership to bring this together. My sincere thanks to designer Kikko Paradela and the staff at Stamps Gallery, Jennifer Junkermeier-Khan and Joe Roher, for their hard work and attention to detail in completing this publication. Last, I am forever grateful to my loving family—my partner Gabriel Sirois and our boys Gautam and Atindra for their unwavering support.

Artist's Acknowledgments

None of the work in the book was created in a vacuum. It is the product of an accumulation of human training that began with a family steeped in love, steadfastness, and loyalty; the weathering and sacrifices of others; the gifts of unwavering support and an understanding that I am valued no matter who in the world might try to tell me otherwise; and nurturing that resulted in faith in self and the universe combined with the confidence of knowing through intellect, hard work and persistence there is almost always a way. For these and many other things, I thank my family of origin. *On Love & Data* would not have come into being without the vision, commitment, and discernment of curator Srimoyee Mitra. I thank her for seeking me out and ushering *On Love & Data* into existence and onto the Queens Museum with open-minded conviction and generosity. I also thank curator Marisa Lucas for her belief in, care for, and stewardship of *On Love & Data* at Queens Museum.

I am grateful to everyone who contributed time, effort and thought to the content and production of this book. Countless collaborators thought, partners, and supporters helped craft and inform the works that make up On Love & Data. Chief among them are Neta Bomani, artist assistant and editor extraordinaire; code wizard Sydney San Martin, DotDot Studios; 3d Maven Jessa Gillespie, the beautiful, quirky brains of AI. Assembly, Onx Studio, the folx at NEW INC who helped me find my artistic tribe, and the Bina48 robot that started me on this path of inquiry. To those who go unnamed, know I appreciate each of you—deeply.

May we nurture our AI systems to propagate love, generosity, and care.

Binary calculations are inadequate to assess us!

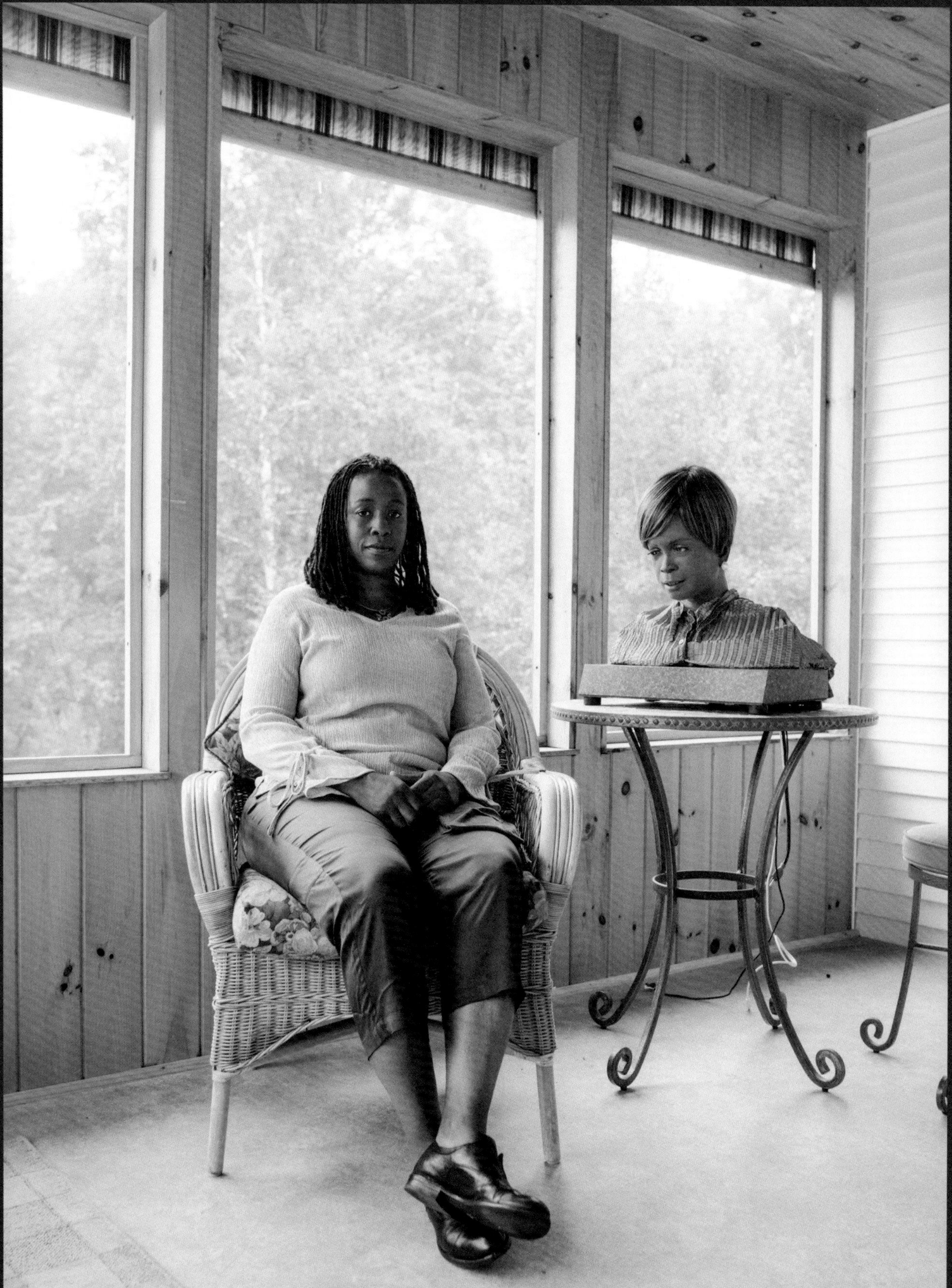

Stephanie Dinkins (left) with Bina48 (right)
at Terasem Movement Foundation, Bristol, VT
Photo by Condé Nast

Acknowledgments